A collection of Mugs

by Paul Flagg

the Peppertree Press LLC
Sarasota, Florida

For information regarding permission,
call 941-922-2662 or contact us at our website:
www.peppertreepublishing.com or write to:
the Peppertree Press, LLC.
Attention: Publisher
1269 First Street, Suite 7
Sarasota, Florida 34236

ISBN: 978-1-61493-772-2

Library of Congress Number: 2021910464

Printed July 2021

To my wife, Ginny

Roberta:

Thirst is eternal.
Your mothers coffee mug
is on Page 21.
Hope everything is going
well,

Paul Haug

Mugs

I cannot possibly cover everything about mugs, because the history of beer goes back thirteen thousand years, with evidence of fermentation found in pottery.

The oldest recorded history of a recipe for beer, using dates, pomegranates, and other herbs, is found on papyrus scrolls dating back five thousand years. However, they were probably not as tasty as today's brews.

That is why this is going to be an abridged version of beer mugs—specifically *my* "collection" in mugs, steins, glasses, and Toby mugs. Otherwise, the subject could literally be volumes. Many of these vessels are simply sold as souvenirs or collectibles and not really used as drinking vessels. What I have found as time goes on is that you cannot drink out of all of the ones you find. However, they have become a collection of fond memories of my times and travels.

Even though beer is considered older than wine in most schools of thought, wine has still brought the greatest price for an aged vessel or container. Not being a wine snob, I have found the rule of thumb here is to find the cheapest wine that you like and stick with it. If you know someone who is a wine snob, give them a choice of your cheap favorite or a high-end bottle. I bet they will not be able to tell the difference. That is all I will say about wine, except that some fancy wine glasses will actually add to the flavor of beer.

Basically, you will find ten different types of beer glasses, although a new one has been added to this selection especially for the ladies. It is known as a schooner and is 25% smaller than the sixteen ounce glass, making it twelve ounces.

1. Pint glasses or shakers are usually sixteen ounces and most commonly used to serve lagers, ales, stouts, porters, and India pale ales (IPAs).

2. Beer mugs come in all sizes and have a handle to keep you from warming your beer or dropping it, if you have had a few too many. Sometimes it will be dimpled, to add to the overall color and clarity of the beer.

3. Steins have a lid and a little lever to lift it. On buggy nights this will keep your beer free of residents doing the back stroke or adding unwanted protein to your beverage. Steins can be made out of pewter, porcelain, stoneware, silver, stainless steel, or wood. The word, *stein*, has been abbreviated from the German word, steinzeug.

Weizen — Strange — Pilsner — Weizen — Strange with a stem

4. Goblets and chalice are somewhat similar. A goblet generally has a long stem with a bowl setting on top. The chalice is basically the same, but with a thicker wall and generally used for Belgian ales and German bock.

5. Pilsner glasses are tall and skinny and designed for—what else—"pilsners." The slightly wider top helps to retain its head, flavor, and aroma.

6. Weizen glass has more curvature than a skinny pilsner to enrich the aromas of IPAs.

7. Snifters are often used with brandies and cognac, but also can be used to enrich the aroma of IPAs. *(none shown here)*

8. Tulip and thistle glasses trap and maintain the foamy head in hoppy and malty brews of Scottish ales. *(none shown here)*

9. Stange glass is not called this because it is strange-looking, but simply *stange* is the German word for *rod*, because the glass is tall and slender

10. Tasting and sample glasses only hold two and a half to six ounces and are designed to do just what it is called—taste or sample beer.

Souvenirs of Corvette — Sampler — Sampler — Regular glass — A Spanish coffee

Another way to buy beer from a brewery is in a glass jug call a *growler*. The only problem with it is that the beer does not stay fresh as long as in a keg. Even though a keg only stays fresh for about a month, the growler goes flat in a day—oh, what a problem!

I have to mention the ubiquitous red—and sometimes blue—plastic drinking vessel used primarily for college parties and lazy bartenders who don't want to wash glasses the next morning. I'll say no more.

To have a great party, I have found that having a variety of mugs and glasses makes it easier for a person to keep track of their vessel. Also, if the guest is a frequent flyer, he or she might have left their own mug or glass in my keeping and then feel even more at home or at ease. An example of this is when I had a friend coming to my home for the first time. After seeing all the different mugs I had, the next time he came over, he brought his skiing mug from Stowe, Vermont.

As I look back on my "collection" of beer mugs, I never thought about collecting them. Whenever, I just ran across one I liked, I just bought it. After I had fifteen or twenty mugs, I kept picking them up on trips to remember the occasion. Only after having acquired fifty or sixty did I start buying them in yard sales or antique stores to add to my collection. After getting upwards of over one hundred and ten of them, I realized I was showing signs of hoarding.

That's when I went through a short period where I bought some license plates for a blank wall, because they were easier to bring home and didn't take up as much room. After realizing that only bars and restaurants should be displaying license plates, I switched to tiny little lapel pins and now that satisfies my collection desires.

However, I still enjoy my mugs and steins—especially my Toby mugs. I look back on my obsession and never regret it. "That's my story and I am stickin' to it."

My first mug was a gift from my wife—a metal mug with a glass bottom to see who was coming at me—this is the legend of glass-bottom mugs. After that, it was a decorative mug with a lid on it to keep out the local bug population while outside. This I heard was the story of why German steins had lids. As I built my first bar, I started picking up glass mugs for easy cleaning and adding to the atmosphere of my bar.

After the first two, I cannot remember the actual sequence of my purchases. However, when I bought my second house, I really had a lot of room in my new bar to display a much larger collection of mugs. Every trip had a mug with my name on it and as friends came to visit, they wanted to have "their" mug hanging on my hooks, also.

I started receiving mugs from the travels of my friends. The strangest of all was when a fellow with whom I worked came to visit me. When he saw my mugs, he brought me a German stein he had found in a farmhouse in Germany in WWII.

One of my friends had a wife who was born in Greece. Every time they went to Greece, they would come back with a Greek mug.

Strangely at Xmas, many friends and family figured that I needed a new mug. Our first wedding present from my wife's family in England was a Toby jug. Her aunt had a collection of them and she said pick whichever one you want. My wife picked Mr. Pickwick. Then I thought it would be nice to buy one every year on our anniversary.

I did not realize that if we were to be married for fifty years, this tradition would become overwhelming. Regrettably, after twelve years, I stopped this little ritual.

As I write about this today, I went online to find Royal Doulton has made over 8,000 caricatures, many of the same people in different poses. Trying to buy all of them is just *not* possible. This is when I realized that I had to stop collecting mugs and steins. As time went on, I also saw there was no way to come even close to having a *complete* collection. That's another reason why this is an *abridged* version of my mug history.

I do enjoy sitting in a room as I write about this collection, remembering my travels, and what each mug represents. I highly recommend mug collecting to anyone with a bar who likes to travel.

Having been in all fifty states, I don't have a mug for each, but I'm sure there is one for every state. It is a little like the RV with a picture of the United States on it—visitors fill in a particular state when they visit it. It does not mean a lot to everyone, except for the person who made those same trips and owns that RV. My mug collection is basically on that same vein.

Ubiquitous- red plastic mug — Souvenirs of Tony's Saloon, Key West
Shaker or Pint — Personal glass mug

My Mug Collection

All pictures will be left to the right unless otherwise stated.

Regular Mug   Flagg Crest   Letter F. for Flagg   Etched sail ship

1 THESE FIRST MUGS ARE EASY BECAUSE THEY CAN BE WASHED.

- This first one is a classic glass mug.
- The second mug in this shot has my family crest with Flagg under it.
- The third mug simply sports an F for Flagg.
- The fourth depicts a fully-rigged ship etched into the glass. There are going to be quite a few nautical mugs, because of my love of the sea and growing up as a Navy brat.

Glass Boot   Black Dog   Bud with Olympic Rings   Watneys

2 THESE NEXT FOUR MUGS HAVE VERY SENTIMENTAL MEMORIES ATTACHED TO THEM.

- The glass boot is different and holds a lot of beer. It reminds me of a song by one of my favorite satirists of popular songs in the mid-twentieth century (Tom Lehrer). His verse was: "Little did I know when I raised that cup, it took two gallons to fill the thing up." I'll change this to: "Little did I know when I raised that cup, it had taken two bottles to fill the thing up."
- The black dog mug comes from a restaurant on Martha's Vineyard and is in memory of my two great beasts, Mac Duff and Ebony. All dogs are great, but those two were, in my eyes, the greatest.
- The Budweiser mug is in commemoration of the Olympics. I cannot remember what year, but I've had it a long time.
- The Watney's mug is for an English beer. Their slogan is, "What we want is Watney's!"

Guinness   Hog Penny Bermuda   Guinness Extra Stout   British with Olympic Rings

3 THE FIRST THREE MUGS ARE DIMPLED TO ENHANCE THE COLOR.

- Both Guinness mugs were made for St. James's Gate Brewery in Dublin, Ireland.
- This Hog Penny mug is from my favorite bar on Bermuda, which is one of my most beloved islands.
- The last mug is a British mug for the Olympics.

Dimpled Mug (Root Beer)   Jar Mug   Montauck Light   German Glass Mug

4 THESE ARE ALL CLASSIC MUGS.

- This is another small, but dimpled mug.
- This jar mug always reminds me of a local watering hole, the Ragged Ass Saloon. They keep one of these mugs available for their special customers.
- This one is shaped like the Montauk Point Lighthouse, which is at the end of Long Island, New York.
- This last one is a German Glass. Not all German drinking vessels are steins.

Souvenir of the Seas — S.S. Norway — O P Sail, Boston — Titanic

5 THESE MUGS ALL RELATE TO MY LOVE OF SAILING.

- This is a mug from Sovereign of the Seas. I really enjoy cruising and I particularly enjoyed this ship.

- The SS Norway was refitted from the SS France and at one time was the largest cruise ship in the world. In its refit, it kept its classic lines. It had the best entertainment of any ship I have ever been on. I particularly remember a show where they were recreating a circus act with a tight rope walker, who was walking over the audience while the ship was rocking and rolling.

- You cannot really see this next mug very well, but it was for a tall ship gathering in Boston called Op Sail. They had over 160 tall ships from all over the world.

- No, I was not on the Titanic, but there is an excellent museum in Branson, Missouri. I also went to a re-creation of the Titanic's last supper in a restaurant in Tyngsboro, Massachusetts called the Left Bank. The restaurant used to be called Silks, because it was also a retirement home for race horses. I guess the Left Bank gave it a more gourmet sounding name. Supper was served along with a PowerPoint presentation on the ship's construction and features. One of the courses served was a single oyster on the half shell—one of my favorite appetizers. My wife had never tried one before, but I encouraged her to sample it and she liked it. I think she did this to keep me from eating hers. Each course was served with a glass of wine that complemented the course. This supper was one of the best I ever had.

Glass mug, small — Anchor — Shower Glass — Tasc 1981 Anniversary

6 THESE ARE ALL DIFFERENT TYPES OF CLASSIC MUGS.

- This is just a simple small mug.
- This one has a nice crystal with an etched anchor.
- This third mug is a rain shower pattern mug.
- This fourth mug is an anniversary mug for TASC. This could stand for "Test Assessing Secondary Completion," which replaced the "General Educational Development" (GED) for the state of New York in 2014. It can also stand for "Transportation Administration Service Center" and the mug is dated 1981 so I'm going with the transportation abbreviation.

English Mugs — Pint to the line — Pint to the brim St. George —Queens Silver Jubilee (1977)

7 ALL FOUR OF THESE MUGS ARE FROM ENGLAND.

- The first two of these have the Queen's measurements on them. It's a form of weights and measures like the US, but we do not control the pour. The first is a pint to the line. The second is a print to the brim with a line on the brim. (not shown)
- The second is a pint to the brim with a line on the brim. The control for whisky is the line, which may be etched, printed, or moulded (and I did not leave out the 'e' in whisky—that's the way the Scots spell whiskey). The English do spell whiskey with an 'e'. For some complicated reason, it is Scottish law to omit the 'e' to tell English whiskey from Scottish whisky. But the reason I digressed is to finish the

English weights and measurements story. Their whiskey is dispensed in optics, so you get an exact pour every time. In all cases, you know you are getting an exact pour. Not like here in the states, where they pour your drink into a shot glass that could have a thick bottom. That's why your bartender might look like he is giving you an extra amount, but he could still be screwing you. I'm sorry I digressed, since my story is about beer. I just had to tell you the weights and measurements story.

- The third mug is a gift from my wife's family in stainless steel with St. George, the dragon slayer's shield.

- The fourth mug celebrates the Queen's silver jubilee in 1977. This means as of this writing, she has been ruling her kingdom for sixty-eight years

Golden Schooner — Treasure Island (at the mirage) — Chesapeake Bay Birds Racing Sail Boats (w/ spinnakers)

8 THIS NEXT MUG IS A GOLDEN SCHOONER.

- The legend of how this sailing vessel received its name is that a young boy was standing on the shore with his father, watching a sailing craft pass by. The boy says to his father, "Daddy, see how she schoons?" The father tells this story to his friends and the rest is myth—or history. The schooner is definitely one of the most practical sailing vessels, because of its ability to be handled by fewer crew members, since it is not square-rigged and will head up into the wind more easily.

This is also a popular vessel for the wealthy, but as a workhorse, it is historic. Schooners that are two-masted up to five-, six- and even seven-masted have hauled coal, timber, and oil. The most famous was the Thomas W. Lawson, named by its owner after himself, and said to be doomed because of the thirteen letters in its name.

It was the only seven-masted schooner ever built, at five hundred feet long and with a steel hull. The masts were generally named fore, main, mizzen, and jigger, but the question was how to name a seven-masted schooner. The simple solution was to call them Monday through Sunday.It was originally designed to haul coal but was converted to carry oil, because of its lack of speed.

On its first trip to England carrying two million gallons of oil, it was hit by three storms. It was disabled off the Scillies Islands southwest of England. This was the largest oil spill occurring up to that date, an unlucky event, even though it had seven masts and was sailing in 1907—the number seven is generally considered lucky. However, because its name had thirteen letters and it went aground on Friday the thirteenth, it was doomed. There are many books written about schooners, but I have always found this one to be fascinating and I had to tell its story.

- The next mug is a souvenir of the Mirage Nightclub in Las Vegas. They used to have a free pirate show out front and staged it on a pirate ship. However, I am told that show stopped in November of 2013.

- The next mug is one covered in sea birds: blue-winged teal, northern pintail, mallard, wood duck, Canada goose, hooded merganser, great blue heron, and the canvasback duck. All of these are birds of Chesapeake Bay, one of my favorite sailing areas with its many coves and rivers to gunk hole in. For those who are not acquainted with this term, it simply means a quaint little spot to drop a hook (anchor), but not to be confused with a hurricane hole, which has more serious requirements, such as having high land to sea ward, having a sandy bottom or marshy shores, and no direct opening to the outer waters.

- The last mug in this group is racing sailboats running with the wind with their spinnakers. Whenever two sailboats get together, it will always be a race.

Cut crystal ship — Dirty Nelly's Pub, San Antonio, Texas — Iranian glass — Small Moxie

9 THESE MUGS ARE *ALL* DIFFERENT.

- This is an etched mug depicting a fully-rigged ship.
- The next mug is from Dirty Nelly's Irish Pub on the Riverwalk in San Antonio, Texas.
- This mug is unusual, because it's from Iran and is made of Iranian glass. I cannot remember how or when I found it, but I have always known it was Iranian.
- This is a Moxie mug and, yes, I know Moxie is not a beer. However, I have always kept it with my beer mugs. If I had not included it with them, it would have felt hurt, left out, and very disappointed.

Burlington H. S. Class of 1929 — Pinkerton Academy
District of Naghoba Regional H. S. Mass. — Lowell H.S. 10th Class Reunion 1968 to 1978

10 THESE REUNION MUGS COMMEMORATE CERTAIN SCHOOLS.

- The one on the left is for the class of 1979 at Burlington High School in Burlington, Massachusetts.

- This one is not a high school, but honors the Pinkerton Academy, which was founded in 1814.

- The one on the right is from the Tenth Class Reunion (1968 to 1978) of the high school in Lowell, Massachusetts.

- The third from the left is from the Nahoba Regional High School, for their 100th anniversary from 1851 to 1951.This high school served the towns of Bolton, Lancaster, and Stow, Massachusetts, which were all in the Nahoba Regional School District. I picked up all of these at yard sales, since I lived near that area.

San Francisco Golden Gate Bridge — Suicide Table Virginia City, Nevada Delta Saloon
Blue Hole, Castalla, Ohio — Niagara Falls

11 THESE NEXT MUGS ARE ALL TRAVEL SOUVENIRS.

- The Golden Gate Bridge is self-explanatory, but everybody should drive over it at least one time in their life, because it's an engineering miracle. At 1.7 miles long and 746 feet high, at the time of its construction in 1937, it was the longest suspension bridge in the world. It goes from San Francisco to Marin County, California. The bridge color is officially called international orange. On its fiftieth anniversary, May 24, 1987, 300,000 people crossed the bridge—it sunk seven feet from the weight. When it had to remove its lead paint and be repainted, it took thirty years. Its fog horns blow on average of two-and-a-half hours every day.

- This next mug was hard to photograph, but it's a souvenir of the Bucket of Blood Saloon in Virginia City, Nevada. That says it all. The saloon was rebuilt in 1876 after the great fire of 1875. It has this charming name, because the owner pulled a bucket of blood out of the well after a murdered smuggler had been dropped into the well with his throat slashed.

- The Blue Hole is in Castalia, Ohio, and is owned by a fishing club. It was open to the public from 1920 to 1990 and is about 75 feet round and 45 feet deep.

- Niagara Falls has been called the honeymoon capital of the world and one of the largest waterfalls in the world, with a height of 167 feet.

Black on white sailing ship — U. S. Constitution — Whale Ship, Gratitude Cruise Ship, Dawn with dolphin

12 THE FIRST MUG IS ALL BLACK ON WHITE. THE NEXT ARE ALL SHIPS. THE LAST ONE IS A CRUISE SHIP.

- This first mug is of the US Constitution. I kept my boat about a quarter mile from where this great vessel is docked. The first time I was on it back in the seventies, they said that it would never sail again. Every Fourth of July it was towed out into Boston Harbor for a turnaround. This is how they evened the weathering effects on the ship. When it was returned to its berth, it would be put back facing the other direction. It was also pulled out every twenty-five years for a complete overhaul.

Then the original blueprints for the vessel were actually found in England showing where its knees (supports) were. The US Records had been lost in time. The powers that be have always kept live oak limbs that had fallen in hurricanes and let them age for any replacement needed in overhauling the Constitution. These limbs were used to restore her likeness to its original construction. Fully restored, this grand old lady was able to sail as she did two hundred years ago for the 200th anniversary of her battle with the British frigate, the HMS Guerriere.

It was said that her sides were like iron, which earned her the nickname, Old Ironsides. She first sailed again on August 19, 2012, but her actual launching for the 200th anniversary was on October 21, 1997.

- This mug is from Bedford, Massachusetts. The whaling ship, Gratitude, was rigged as a bark, a three-masted vessel with square sails on her fore and mainmasts. This was done to some ships to cut down on how many crewmembers were needed to handle the sails., The Gratitude went to the Pacific ten times, from 1831 to 1865.

- The most famous whaling ship was the Charles W. Morgan, which is still docked in Mystic, Connecticut. One of 2700 whaling ships, the Morgan is the oldest commercial ship still afloat.

- This is a mug from the Norwegian Dawn, a ship in the Norwegian Cruise Lines (NCL). We sailed out of Boston, Massachusetts, although its other port is Tampa, Florida. We went to my favorite island, Bermuda, and docked in the old navy base my father used to go to in his navy days. The ship is well equipped with three pools, seven Jacuzzis, twelve elevators, and eleven lounges and has fifteen dining options. It has the capacity to carry 2,340 passengers.

Norman Rockwell Lg. Model Maker — Small Model Maker —Old Salt in Storm
The Freedom Train

13 THESE NEXT MUGS WERE EXAMPLES OF NORMAN ROCKWELL'S ART.

- This first one is a large mug, a model maker with a parrot.
- This one is a small Norman Rockwell mug, a model maker with a parrot.
- This last one is a small Norman Rockwell of an old salt in a storm.
- The Freedom train toured the country in the mid-seventies. One mug even commemorated the Freedom train. My verse to this occasion:

> *Sometimes simple*
> *Sometimes plain.*
> *The Freedom Train*

Mount Rushmore — Grand Canyon — Route 66 Barstow, California — Alaska

14 ALL FOUR OF THE FOLLOWING MUGS ARE TRAVEL SOUVENIRS.

- I should have put this first one with my Chief Crazy Horse mug, because Mt. Rushmore and the Crazy Horse carving are only 17 miles apart; but I put it with three others because of their colors.

Mt. Rushmore is a massive sculpture carved into the mountain in the black hills of South Dakota. It is sixty feet high and each nose is twenty feet long. Under the direction of sculptor Gutzon Borglum and his son, Lincoln. This project was started on October 4, 1927 and completed October 31, 1941.The four presidents are George Washington, Thomas Jefferson, Theodore Roosevelt, and Abraham Lincoln. These four are often considered our greatest presidents. The one thing a lot of people do not know is that a tunnel was created in back of it to a secret room that explains the history of the sculpture for future visitors.

- The Grand Canyon cannot be covered in a couple of sentences. However, having hiked to the bottom twice, I recommend that this is another spot that should be visited at least once by all Americans, even if they just stand at the rim and look in.

My brother-in-law said to me as we approached the rim for my first time, "This will be a view that you will never forget." He was right, even though we were in a cloud bank and the visibility was about one hundred feet. I still do not let him forget that statement.

As we were starting in, we listened to a mule skinner give an short explanation to all tourists who were about to take the mule ride into the canyon. He remarked that when the caravan stopped or if the view over the edge got too scary, just close our eyes—that's what the mules do.

The strangest thing of all was that the temperature was in the twenties, but as we descended it got warmer and warmer, so at the bottom, it was in the mid-seventies. You literally go through all the climates of the northern hemisphere in your hike into the canyon. We started with three inches of snow and ice and wearing ice cleats, but we had to strip down to just a shirt at the bottom and this was February. In the summer, the park rangers do not let you go down without a gallon of water, as the temperature can climb well over 100 degrees.

- Route 66 is part of my childhood memories, because my father was stationed on the West Coast before I was six. I remember crossing the desert with water bags strapped to the fenders. And in the mountains when it dropped below 32 degrees, he would drain the water in the engine and put it back in the morning before we left. The most memorable thing I remember was the locust infestation at a gas station with a three-holer in back for a toilet. I think it was in Kansas. I purchased the mug in my adult travels.

  Michael Wallis has written an excellent book about Route 66 called *The Mother Road*.

- Everybody knows about Alaska. I saw Alaska on a cruise out of Vancouver British Columbia, Canada. This is a cruise everybody should take once in their life on the inland passage where it is very protected and it can't get more scenic. The best time to go is September, because there is less fog and the temperature is mild for Alaska (mid-fifties to mid-sixties) and it rains only about six days out of the month. The White Pass and Yukon Railway were incredible.

Budweiser — Busch Gardens, Clydesdales — Save the Bay — Logo on Glass

15 THERE ARE MANY BUDWEISER MUGS, BUT HERE ARE SOME OF MINE.

- The first is from Busch Gardens, an amusement park in Williamsburg, Virginia. However, there is also a park in Tampa, Florida.

- The Clydesdales are kept at St. Louis, Missouri; Merrimack, New Hampshire; and Fort Collins, Colorado. All the hitch horses are geldings, but there are over one hundred kept at Warm Springs Ranch, which is a breeding farm on three hundred plus acres of lush, rolling hills in the heart of Missouri. This was established in 2008 and features a mare/stallion and foaling barn, veterinary lab, and ten pastures, each with a customized walk-in shelter. Anheuser-Busch owns about two hundred fifty Clydesdales around the country.

- This mug portrays how Budweiser helped to save Narragansett Bay from pollution. Storm water with tons of sewage was being dumped into the bay that is located on the north side of Rhode Island Sound.

- This last mug is just a regular drinking mug.

Gold Sailing Ship — U.S.S. Missouri — Windjammer— Elizabeth II, Roanoke

16 THE FOLLOWING SHIPS ARE ALL HISTORIC MASTERPIECES.

- Here is another gold ship under full sail. What a beauty!

- You may not be able to see that this mug is about the USS Missouri firing its 16-inch guns, 65 feet long and weigh 116 tons each. It is an Iowa-class battleship, one of four in this class. It was launched January 29, 1944 and decommissioned on March 13, 1992. It is now open to the public at Pearl Harbor in Oahu, Hawaii. It's most famous for being the ship where the signing of the surrender of Japan occurred at the end of WWII.

- This one is a pewter mug from our windjammer cruise. The vessel shown here is a square-rigged ship, but our cruise was on a four-masted schooner. It was a converted Portuguese fishing vessel named Argus, but renamed Polynesia as a windjammer. It was 248 feet long with a beam of 36 feet and a draft of 18 feet. It was taken out of service in 2007, but returned to the Portuguese as a training ship for Portuguese youth and renamed Argus.

- Elizabeth II is a historic recreation of Sir Walter Raleigh's 69-foot vessel that carried the first English colonists to the New World in 1585 with seven other vessels.

German Scene — Clyde, Ohio — Cigar Store Indian — Stowe, Vermont

17

- This a German mug—not a stein. If you look closely, you'll see there is no lid and it has a quaint German scene on it.

- Clyde, Ohio, is home to some of my wife's family and to the world's largest washing machine plant (Whirlpool). It also houses President Rutherford B. Hayes' Library and Museum.

- This one is a simple mug of a cigar store Indian. Some people wonder why the Indians are connected with tobacco. It's simple—the Indians introduced the Europeans to tobacco.
- This last one is the ski mug that a friend brought, so he would have a mug at my bar. My wife asked if this meant he was coming back, because she did not particularly like him. She gets upset when I tell this story. I always get a kick out of telling it, because her wit can be very sharp.

Shriner Mug — American Eagle — Sears Tower —Power Squadron, 85ʰ Anniversary

18 THREE OF THESE MUGS ARE BASICALLY MY LIFE'S STORY.

- I have been a Shriner for almost fifty years and this mug reminds me of the poor children who are so severely burned they need skin grafts or prosthetics. The Shrines take care of them until their adult years, age 18. There is a change of philosophy coming now that if a child has insurance, they will ask if the insurance company can help. Still, no money will be requested from the parents. When I joined, part of the day's ceremony included a trip to the closest Shriner hospital. For me it was the Shriner burns center in Boston, Massachusetts, to see what your time and money went toward. I will never forget the little guy lying in bed with his face so severely burned you could see his cheekbone. When you entered his room, his face lit up with a smile. A friend of mine had a prosthetic leg and I asked her if the Shiners had helped with the loss of her leg. She said they took care of everything up until she was eighteen. She lost her leg when she was two. There are twenty-two Shriner hospitals dedicated to burns or prosthetics around the country.
- This mug is a bit different from the rest. However, I am not sure where I got this blue eagle or why it's in this group. But it appealed to me.
- The third mug from the left is from the Sears Tower. Having worked for Sears for thirty-four years, I had always wanted to go up to the top. The tower was started in 1970 and completed in May 1973. It was 1,450 feet high and with its broadcasting antennas, it was 1,729 feet, making it the world's tallest building for twenty-five years. It was sold to Willis Group Holdings and Sears moved its corporate offices to Hoffman Estates outside of Chicago. It was then sold to Blackstone for 1.3 billion dollars in 2015. I retired from Sears in 1998 and went on to work at Homelife, a subsidiary of Sears, for another six years. I finished my career with seven years at Bob's Discount Furniture Store. However, my early days with Sears is where I met many lifelong friends.

- The last mug is from the Power Squadron, which kept me busy for forty-five years. This organization helped me obtain my captain's license and I also met lifetime friends with similar interest from this organization whose goal it is to teach safe boating and navigation. When I became a member of what they call The Bridge, I traveled all over the US three times a year, making new friends and visiting interesting cities. I always made sure to leave a couple of days on either side of their national meetings to see the sights of each area. This is where I picked up a lot my mugs.

Devon, England — I am not a gossip — Reno, Nevada —Camel mug or cup

19 THESE NEXT MUGS ARE FROM AREAS THAT ARE NOT NEAR EACH OTHER.

- You cannot really see this mug very clearly of the Devon in the southwest corner of England. It reaches from Bristol Channel in the north to the English Channel in the south. Devon is renowned for its spectacular coast and its Devonshire cream. It is about one hundred ninety miles from London, but seems more remote.

- I like what this next mug says: "I am not a gossip. I just happen to be gifted with a keen sense of rumor."

- Reno, Nevada, has the claim of being the biggest little city. I found that it has a fantastic automobile museum, The Nevada Museum of Art, a fantastic planetarium and, if you are there at the right time, hot-air balloon races. Do not try driving when watching the balloon races. I could not believe how many cars were going off the road watching the balloons. As I was leaving Reno, I see a balloon off in the distance and as I am watching, somebody jumps out of the balloon. What I could not see was the bungee cord connected to the jumper. This is something I will always remember. I have related this story to people that I have known that are bungee jumpers. They told me the problem with jumping out of a hot-air balloon is you must know your altitude is such that you have enough room to bounce. If you have a problem with getting things right the first time. Bungie jumping is not for you.

- I have to confess that this Camel mug was given to me from my cousin. It was really her mother's coffee mug, but it was large enough to be considered a beer mug and she wanted it to go into my collection as a beer mug in memory of her mother, my Aunt Hazel.

Wall Darug — Nova Scotia— University of NewHampshire 1923
Red Sox World Series win 2004

20 THESE MUGS ALL HONOR HISTORICAL HAPPENINGS, LIKE WALL DRUG STORE.

- In 1931, Ted Hustead and his wife, Dorothy, bought a drug store and struggled for five years with very little business. Then one hot summer day Dorothy came up with the idea of offering free ice water to hot and thirsty travelers. The rest is history and from that day on Wall, South Dakota, became famous attracting two million visitors a year and they are still offering free ice water—even though my mug is for beer.

- This mug I found in Nova Scotia, host of the *Curse of Oak Island* on the History Channel and my Uncle's Murry's birthplace. When I went to visit his old neighbors, I stopped and asked a lady walking down the street knew John Coldwell. She was a little suspicious until I told her who I was. She said John was retired now, though he never did much of anything and then she gave me directions. As I pull up, the chickens are flying in and out of the windows and a goat is walking out the kitchen door. I visited for a while then I said I would like to get a photo for my uncle. John's wife said, "Wait a minute! I have to change." This made sense to me, seeing that she had a three-corner tear on the left breast of her dress. She comes back in a few minutes with the same dress on. Seeing the quizzical look on my face she simply said, "I had on John's boots." Yes, Nova Scotia is a laid-back province—at least, I hope it still is. This all took place fifty-five years ago.

- Another time I was up there and pumping gas. Suddenly, a woman next to me starts excitingly to tell the gas station attendant, "Cabin is coming today!" We pull out and go around a corner and here comes a cabin taking up most of the road, with a very excited lady waiting for it.

- This mug from the University of New Hampshire is dated 1923.

- Living outside of Boston most of my life, I always heard, "Wait till next year for the Red Sox to win the pennant." They finally did in 2004.

Dr. Bird — 5 cent Beer — U.S. Light House Services — English Pub, Miami, Florida

21 THESE MUGS ARE ALL FROM MEMORABLE LOCATIONS.

- The Dr. Bird mug is in memory of my visit to Jamaica. The swallow-tail hummingbird is Jamaica's national bird—its Latin name is trochilus polytmus. It supposedly gets its name from its plumage, which resembles a doctor's coat and hat. Some say that Dr. Bird is an imaginary pigeon therapist.

- Five Cents a Beer is the slogan for this next mug. I can't even remember when beer was that cheap.

- The National Light House Service was founded in 1910 and replaced by the United States Coast Guard in 1939. With the abolishment of the service, all lighthouses were manned by the first guard up to 1996, when almost all of them became automated. The exception was the Boston Light, which was manned for a time by an acquaintance of mine and his dog.

  The first lighthouses were built around the thirteenth century and some were actually Christian monasteries. The oldest lighthouse is said to be Hook Lighthouse in Hook Head at the tip of the Hook Peninsula in County Wexford, in Ireland, built in the early twelve hundreds.

  An interesting story about lighthouses comes from Key West. Salvage outfits operated under a license by federal court, which journalist Hunter S. Thompson described it as the "cruel imperatives of salvaging rights." This meant whoever got to the cargo first and could defend it with any form of weapon or sheer strength had the rights to it. These people were called wreckers, because they would tear down lighthouses and put up phony light signals to cause a shipwreck.

- The last mug here is the English Pub out of Miami, Florida. It has a little verse on the back: Honor, fame, love, and wealth may desert us, but thirst is eternal.

22 THE FIRST TWO ITEMS IN THIS SECTION ARE NOT MUGS.

- This one is billed as a perfect pair, but look closely—it already has a match that would make it part of a perfect pair. I just figured out that it has to be put next to my mug from St. Maarten for the man who enjoys and likes to suckle his beer.

- This next one is also not a mug, but a prohibition bottle from Harvard Brewery, located in Lowell, Massachusetts. They thought that if they could export their beer, they could stay in business. However, this did not happen.

A Perfect Pai...Pear — St, Marten — Harvard Beer quart —Lowell Souvenir

- I ended up working on the property where the brewery was located, as one of my first jobs with Sears. Then in my final years of employment, I worked for Bob's Discount Furniture, which was located in the old warehouse of the brewery.
- The last item is a souvenir mug from Lowell, Massachusetts.

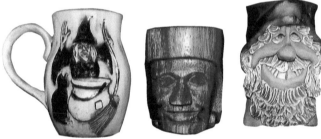

The Witch and her court

23 BEWARE THIS MUG!

- This witch's curse can change you into any likeness.

24 THIS NEXT MUG STARTS IN CEDAR POINT, OHIO.

- It is an amusement park in northern Ohio and where my (follow me on this one) brother-in-law's son's wife works in the office. The night I went there was just before Halloween. I asked her how many people had entered today. She checked and told me the gate had counted 43,000, but the maximum capacity is 55,000. They were there to ride some of the tallest roller coaster rides in the world with eighteen from which to choose.

Cedar Point — Chesapeake Bay Bridge & Tunnel — Pelee Point & Canada
Old Sturbridge Village

- One roller coaster is 420 feet tall and can reach speeds of 120 miles per hour. Being on Lake Erie, they sometimes have to shut them down due to high winds, rain, or lighting. What I found fascinating is they are required to have people climb each of them every day and check them out before they are put into service. I do know my roller coaster days are over, but I could not ride a lot of these coasters—even in my younger days.

- This next mug commemorates the Chesapeake Bay Bridge/Tunnel, which to me is an engineering marvel. I remember my first passage across the bay by ferry was in 1948 in a storm. The man standing next to me had his rosary beads clutched tightly in his fists. The bridge construction started in October 1960 and was completed in April 1964. It is 17.6 miles long and one of only eleven bay bridge tunnels in the world. It allows any size ship or aircraft carrier to enter the Chesapeake Bay and go into the navy yard in Norfolk ,Virginia, or go up to Baltimore, Maryland.

- Pelee Island, Ontario, Canada, is in Lake Erie and the southernmost point of Canada. That is actually Middle Island, which is part of Pelee Island township. This point is below or partially below 27 states in the US. Pelee Island has a population of 300 year-round residents, but this number swells to 1,500 in the summer. In autumn, Monarch butterflies mass here in the thousands, waiting for the right conditions to cross Lake Erie and migrate to Mexico. How those little guys know when the conditions are right is beyond me, but it might have something to do with a tailwind.

- When I arrived in Pelee at 3:45 p.m., there was a sign indicating that to be cleared into Canada, I had to call Customs at a given phone number. The Customs officer would be there at 4:00 p.m. Well, I figured I would just wait till 4:00 p.m. and not call. When four o'clock comes, this 18-year-old girl in a uniform approaches me and asked if I had called Customs when I arrived. I said I just figured, you'd be here in fifteen minutes, so I would wait and report in when you came at 4:00 p.m. She exploded and threatened to lock me up, because I had not called when I arrived. I apologized, but cooler heads prevailed, so I got off with a warning. You could tell she really enjoyed this position of authority.

- This last mug is from Old Sturbridge Village, which is a living museum that recreates life in rural New England during the 1790s through 1830. It is the largest living museum in New England, covering more than two hundred acres.

Rope Mug — Quartet — Irish Mug —Young Salt

25 MY WIFE MADE ALL FOUR OF THESE MUGS IN HER CERAMIC CLASS.

- The rope mug
- The Quartet
- The Irish mug with a leprechaun for a handle
- The young salt (not an old salt).

She refers to this as her ceramic period of life.

26 THE FIRST TWO OF THESE MUGS WERE ALSO MADE BY MY WIFE.

- This first one is very plain, except for the fancy writing on it of our family name, Flagg.
- The one in the middle is her largest, a tall Xmas mug.
- The far right one is her favorite. It was probably made for a woman, because it is a Limoges mug from France.

Large Flagg — Christmas Stein —Limonge

27 THESE NEXT MUGS MAY GENERATE A SURPRISE.

- Blow your horn or ring a bell for a beer. When you get the beer, look out for who is coming at you with a gun.

Blow your Horn or Ring your Bell for a Beer
Watch to see who is coming at you with a gun

Copper — LL Bean — Stootgunshell — Brass Indian Mug – (Dot not Feather)

28 SEVERAL DIFFERENT TYPES OF MUGS ARE IN THIS SECTION.

- Copper mugs are displayed on each end of this segment.
- An LL Bean shotgun shell mug with a pheasant on the wing is in the center.
- Last in this group is an Indian mug (the Indians who have a dot on their forehead, not a feather in their hair). The pattern is lost in this photo but it is a very nice one.

White on White — On the ends — Biker mug —Michelob

29 THESE FOLLOWING MUGS HAVE BEEN WITH ME A LONG TIME.

- The mugs on each end are raised white scenes on white.
- The second from the left is a 2005 monkey bar Harley. This shot does not do it justice, because the shot wraps all around the mug.
- This is a Michelob mug, which I trust needs no explanation.

Crazy Horse — Duck — Racing Sailboats —Sailboat w/ spinnaker under rainbow

30 THESE FOUR MUGS GO TOGETHER, DUE TO THEIR VARIETY OF COLOR.

- I have said that I should have put the Crazy Horse mug with the Mt. Rushmore mug, because they are only seventeen miles apart in the Black Hills of South Dakota. It is a memorial being built by Korczak Zielkowski's family. Korczak was the artist and creator of Mt. Rushmore. His son is now carrying the torch for the Crazy Horse completion. When completed, it will be considered the eighth wonder of the world and will be the largest mountain carving in the world. It's being done with no government money. It will depict the Oglala Lakota Warrior, Crazy Horse, pointing to his tribal land, which was the Lakota's long before the Pilgrims landed at Plymouth Rock. The height will be 564 feet and the length 640 feet. It's already been under construction for over seventy years.

- The mallard seen here is the male. Like most birds, the male is the colorful one and is called a drake. The female is brown-speckled and is called a hen. They are both known as "dabbling ducks," because of their tipping forward and grazing on underwater plants. If tamed, they can actually make good pets and can live up to ten years. They would come to me on the pond I lived on and I always enjoyed their company.

- These racing sailboats remind me of my younger years when I was more agile.

- This last mug under the rainbow also brings back memories of my younger years.

31 MY LIFE IS REFLECTED IN MANY OF THESE MUGS.

- Pawleys Island was established in 1740 and is seventy miles north of Charleston, South Carolina, where I lived as a child in the early 1950s. It is very close to Brookgreen Gardens, which has to be one of the nicest gardens in our country with fantastic sculptures and a zoo. It is near Huntington Beach, home to Atalaya, a Moorish-style mansion.

- I was at meetings in Philadelphia, when there was strong rumors of the Eagles leaving Philadelphia. I went into a store and saw this mug for sale. I told the

Pauley's Island, 1740 S.C. — Philadelphia Eagles — Roman — Your father's mustache

clerk that I would take the mug, because it will be a collector's item shortly. He gave me a very dirty look, but sold it to me anyhow. Fortunately, the Eagles did not leave and I still have the mug, but not a collectible as I had planned.

- The Romans were probably one of the greatest civilizations in history. I cannot remember where I got this mug, but it might have been at the Roman Baths in Bath, Somerset, England.

- Your father's mustache bar on Bourbon Street, New Orleans, was a great bar. You can't see it at this angle, but there is a mustache guard on the rim of the mug.

Worn Girls School Nahoba Regional H.S.   1951…25 years
Nantucket Whaling —English Scene

32 THESE MUGS HOLD SEVERAL FOND MEMORIES FOR ME.

- The blue mug was from a girls' school, but you can barely read the school's name. I bought it at a yard sale and the girls must have liked their beer, because almost all the lettering is worn off. Maybe they just washed it a lot.

- This Nahoba mug looked the same as another of my pictures. When I looked for what happened, I found I had two of them. I had never matched them up to realize I had two.

- The Nantucket whaling mug was from their museum of which a friend was the curator. For a while, he had whale oil for lamps. He told me they had found a dead whale that they had drug into an enclosure in a cove for the crabs to pick clean. Then they brought the skeleton into the museum and hung it from the ceiling.

- This last mug is a depiction of a quaint English scene of the old coach house in Woolhampton, England.

Beige/gold —Bucket of Blood Saloon —Roque River — Okefenokee Swamp

33 THESE NEXT MUGS ARE STRANGELY DIFFERENT.

- I just like the beige and gold colors of this mug. I bought it, because I didn't have any like it.

- This is another mug from the "Bucket of Blood Saloon." They had a gaming table inside called a Suicide Table. This table gained its "pleasant" name when three of its previous owners committed suicide after losing at a game of cards.

- The Rogue River is one of the longest in Oregon and is very scenic. Its source is high in the Cascade Mountains near Crater Lake. It flows more than two hundred miles to enter the Pacific Ocean at Gold Beach through Grants Pass. This is a very scenic river that ends where some of my old neighbors moved.

- Okefenokee Swamp is a shallow 438,000-acre wetlands area, which was designated as a World Heritage site in 1974. Almost undisturbed for centuries with its seven hundred square mile area, it is the largest swamp in North America. Its population is primarily alligators, turtles, herons, bitterns, flycatchers, ibises, and many more waterfowl.

Elephant handled — For all I do — Christmas — Black on white sailing ship

34 THE NEXT MUG IS SIMILAR TO THE ONES IN #12 OF MY COLLECTION.

- This mug is perfectly plain, except that the head of an elephant is the handle.

- Every bar should have one of these mugs just to show our appreciation for customers. Here's to you all!

- This is an Xmas mug with Xmas munchkins looking out the window into the cold. Holly trims the top and bottom and also the handle.

- Yes, this is another full-rigged black on white ship running with the wind. It's just a little different than the other ship in #12 of my collection.

Prince of Fundy— Mykonos, Greek — Castle Harbor, Bermuda — Plain Mug

35 MANY OF MY MUGS ARE HISTORICAL IN NATURE.

- This mug is from the Prince of Fundy. I googled its history and that of the ferry service from Maine to Nova Scotia. It appears to be more complicated than I thought. The Prince ran from 1970 to 1976. Next, the ferry service picked up with the Scotia Prince, and then the Cat came on the scene with a quick crossing of three and a half hours, as opposed to the sluggardly older passage of time of eleven hours. I believe that they both had gambling so I know that people took this passage back and forth just to gamble. The cat's berth at this writing is in Charleston, South Carolina.

- The Mykonos mug is from friends that visited this Greek island. I am told that it is beautiful. It is located in the Aegean Sea and known for its great beaches, picturesque villages, delicious Greek food, and great night life.

- This mug is from the Castle Harbour Hotel in Bermuda that closed in 1984 and reopen as Tucker's Point Marriott Hotel in 1986. It continued till 1999 and reopened again 2009 with 88 rooms instead of 402, as the Rosewood Hotel and Resorts. I will always remember it as Castle Harbour with one of the greatest bars I had ever been in. Where the bartenders stood was recessed, so if you were sitting in their Queen Anne high wing-backed chairs, you were looking the bartenders right in the eye. Behind them was a mural of two galleons during a tumultuous sea battle. A cannon was up in one corner of the bar.

- This one is just a plain dark mug with no story.

36 YOU'LL NOTICE QUITE A BIG DIFFERENCE IN THE MUGS IN THIS SECTION.

- This one is a replica of a Pilgrim's drinking mug. I wrote the last verse of my poem found at the end of this book when I first saw this mug: "The pilgrim's mug is made from leather What did the Indians use that wore a feather?"

- The mug from Arizona reminds me of a sign at the Phoenix airport. The Sky Harbor International Airport had to suspend some flights because of the heat. However, as they say, "it's a dry heat."

Replica mug, Pilgrim leather — Arizona — Playboy — Small Metal Mug

- I was not a member of the Playboy Club, but I had a friend who belonged. I picked up this mug on one of our visits there. I was there once during a fire drill, so we all had to go outside. The bunnies had to get out of their uniform, which meant they had to remove their little white bunny tails.

- *The last mug in this group may seem small, but it is one of my heaviest, since it's made out of metal.

Squat Ale mug — Rock Point School for Girls — San Francisco Golden Gate Bridge
Ancient Greek

37 THIS IS ANOTHER GROUP OF SMALL MUGS.

- This first one is a German mug. All you can see in this shot is *alle*, but on each side of the handle are the words *gut* and *holz*. In German, *holz* means wood and *gut* means good. There are other meanings for these words, but these make the most sense. This is a bowling mug from Gerz.

- This is a girl's mug for Rock Point School in Burlington, Vermont. It is considered a preparatory and boarding school. At this writing, it has fourteen students and was founded in 1928.

- This is another mug from San Francisco, similar to the one that is in the set on Print #11.

- This is another mug brought back by my friends who like to visit Greece.

German Officer Club 1958 — For the two-fisted drinker — Stoneware mug — Relaxing mug

38 HERE'S ANOTHER GROUPING OF SIMPLE MUGS.

- This first one is from an officer's club in Ramstein-Miesenbach, Germany. I don't remember where I got it from, since I was not there.
- As you can see, this mug is for the two-fisted drinker.
- This one is just a simple stoneware mug.
- Here's a relaxing mug of glass with a wooden handle.

39 THIS NEXT ONE IS REALLY A WINE BOTTLE HOLDER.

- The neck of the bottle goes to the duck's mouth with the base of the bottle being held by the webbed feet. However, if you look closely, I thought that you would see that it would demonstrate a slight problem. It seems that once beer was poured into this mug, the drinker could not sit it down until it was finished.

Mug… you can't sit down
Till your beer is finished

40 THESE LAST PRINTS ARE QUITE VARIED.

- Remember the WWII vet I mentioned in my intro to this book? That wasn't the whole story. He came home one day to find his wife had put his German stein up for sale for one dollar in a yard sale. This is that very same mug. He wanted it to have a good home and he knew where it was. It was his to give away—not hers to sell for a dollar.
- This next mug has all the NFL football teams on it. I have four of them, but the other three are full of stirrers from cocktail days in New England and my travels.

WWII German Stein

NFL Helmets — Aztec or Mayan —121ˢᵗ Kentucky Derby — NASA

- I cannot say where I got this mug, but it is proof that when you collect a mug, you should write a little note and put it in the mug. I cannot remember where I got it from and whether it is Aztec or Mayan. I believe I got it in Belize.

- The 121st Kentucky Derby was on May 6, 1995. The winning horse was Thunder Gulch with 144,110 in attendance. The Kentucky Derby creates a mug every year, but this was the only derby I ever attended.

- I bought this mug at NASA in Cape Canaveral, but I have also gone through the museum at Huntsville, Alabama—both are fantastic.

Baseball — Wild West — Sportsman

- Some Avon beer steins were originally sold just as steins. Others came with Avon's popular cologne inside. This first one for 1984 portrays baseball uniforms from 1900, 1920, 1940, and from 1960, to 1980. The top of the stein is a glove and its handle replicates the stitches of a baseball.

- The next Avon stein from 1980 represents the Wild West. It depicts a cattle drive, a stage coach, roping, a chuck wagon, and a rope handle.

- This last Avon stein from 1978 is for the sportsman. One scene is a fisherman showing the strike of a rainbow trout. For the hunter, there's an English setter on point for a pheasant.

The next five prints are of all my steins. There are literally thousands and I only show them here, because they are all beer-related and originally came from Germany. After WWII, many Germans escaped and went to South America, primarily Brazil, and continued their craft there. I don't drink out of them—I just like them as atmosphere and art. The lid on beer steins was a sanitary measure to keep out plague germs and insects. They're usually equipped with a lever to reach with a thumb to open the lid with a single hand. A stein is usually made of ceramic, while a tankard is made out of pewter. (A German beer stein may also be called a Bierkrug.)

John Deer — Trains — Indians

41 THESE AVON MUGS CELEBRATE FAMOUS ITEMS AND HISTORICAL EVENTS.

- John Deere's green and gold logo is displayed on this Avon replica of their famous tractor beer stein.
- This mug commemorates the completion of Richard Trevithick's locomotive in February of 1804.

    *The General beer stein commemorates the locomotive that was built in 1855 and commandeered by northerners during the Civil War. For many years, the General was on display in the Chattanooga Union Depot. Today, it resides in the Big Shanty Museum, which is now known as the Southern Museum of Civil War and Locomotive History.

- This 1982 Avon beer stein portrays the Orient Express, Age of the Iron Horse of 1925. This vintage Avon ceramic beer lidded-stein is made by Avon to represent the 1938 Twentieth Century train.

    In 1985, Avon created the Union Pacific Railroad beer stein to celebrate its original creation in 1941.

- Avon handcrafted this stein in Brazil in 1988, as a remembrance of Indians of the American Frontier.

Large old cars — Small old cars — Large ships —Small ships

42 AVON LARGE AND SMALL (NO LID) MUGS REPLICATE CARS AND SHIPS:

- This Avon beer stein has a wrap-around parade of the 1910 Stanley Steamer, 1911 Ford Model-T, 1936 MG, and the 1927 Bugatti. It was handcrafted in Brazil exclusively for Avon Products, Inc. in1979 and made by Ceramarte in Brazil. It reminds me of the 17 Stanley Steamers i saw running in Marietta, Ohio.

- This Avon Vintage Beer Stein was made in 1977, and is surrounded by tall ships. It features a jib-headed ketch, a barkentine, a brigantine, a bark, a staysail, and a schooner. At nine inches tall, it is numbered and was made in Brazil by Ceramarte.

Alaskan animals & birds — Football uniforms — Large planes — Small planes

43 THIS SEGMENT IS A MIXED BAG OF AVON STEINS.

- Avon created some beautiful steins of Alaskan animals and birds:Rocky Mountain Goat, Condor, Bighorn Sheep, Alaskan Moose, Falcon.

- Avon also created steins for certain football uniforms:1900, 1920, 1940,1960,1980.

- These Avon steins commemorate both large and small planes and a hot-air balloon: 1903 Wright Brothers, 1909 Bleriot,1927 Ford Tri Motor,1930 Waco Biplane,1931 Sikorsky Sea Plane, 1940 Piper Cub, 1783 Montgolfier hot-air balloon.

Regular stein — Regular stein — Ship stein — VIP stein

44 THIS SECTION OF STEINS HAS SOME MYSTERY ELEMENTS TO IT.

- This German zahle stein translates to: "I'll pay!"

  *Under the handle of this next stein is a German quote: Ein volles glas des spass, which means "When the glass is full, the guests are thrilled."

- This next is a mystery as there is nothing on it, but a beautiful picture of a fully-rigged ship running with the wind with all sails set. I do not know where I got it or its country of origin. Because it is a stein, I am assuming it is German, but I cannot say for sure. I can say this would make an incredible picture. I have an oil painting that is similar, but not quite as nice as this.

- This is another mystery stein that is all glass in a deep cobalt blue. It has no markings indicating the country of origin, but the Germans do like this color. The cobalt blue is used by the German stein maker, Gers. Also, a seal on this mug has a VIP in the middle of it and on the back is a poem I have heard before. It's called: "Love" or "The Greatest Love of All." I have tried to verify the poet's name, but I found that the experts disagree. Either the poet is anonymous or perhaps General Louis H. Wilson wrote it. You have probably heard it yourself:

> *"The wonderful love of a beautiful maid,*
> *The love of a staunch true man,*
> *The love of a baby, unafraid,*
> *Have existed since time began.*
>
> *But the greatest of loves, The quintessence of loves.*
> *even greater than that of a mother,*
> *Is the tender, passionate, infinite love,*
> *of one drunken Marine for another.*
> *"Semper Fidelis"*

—General Louis H. Wilson

Gerz old German with fox handle — Avon African Serangeti — Barrel Chested Gerz pitcher

45 GERZ STEIN COMPANY CREATED VARIED ARTISTIC STEINS.

- This German mug has a fox handle. The hunting scene is labeled, "Waidmanns Heil," which translates to "Good Hunting."

- The next one is produced by Avon. It's a 2005 stein depicting Africa's Serengeti, which spans northern Tanzania.

- Gerz created this mug, but it's really more of a pitcher than a stein, because it has a spout.

Flaxman pitcher, Greek Revival — German with Swiss Scene — Budweiser – black dog
Whale tale mug

46 THIS NEXT PRINT CONTAINS A DIVERSE GROUPING.

- This Greek Revival pitcher was created by sculptor and illustrator, John Flaxman.

- The next German stein has no mark.

- Budweiser Beer created this black dog stein. I have these in memory of two great dogs in my life, MacDuff and Ebony.

- This next offering is not a stein, but an unusual mug with a whale's tail for a handle. Toby caricature, of which over 8,000 have been created. Many have the same person on several different mugs. They are made to be decorative, even though they are called mugs.

Old Salt — Small Bacchus — St. George — Robin Hood

47 THESE THREE MUGS WERE CREATED TO REPRESENT SOME FAMOUS PEOPLE.

- The old salt allows you to hang on to your beer with its mermaid handle.
- The St. George mug pays tribute to the patron saint of England.
- Robin Hood is famous in England for robbing from the rich and giving to the poor.

Flastaff — Small Don Quixote — Auld Mac — Small the Stuth
Catherine of Aragon — Old Charlie

48 YOU'LL SEE SOME FAMOUS FICTIONAL NAMES AMONG THESE STEINS.

- This large 1949 Royal Doulton mug depicts Falstaff, a fictional character who appears in three plays by William Shakespeare.
- This small Toby 1956 mug creates the character of Don Quixote, who attempts to revive chivalry and tilts at windmills.
- Auld Mac is a vintage Royal Doulton miniature sailor with a weathered face and a lop-sided grin.
- This small Royal Doulton mug made in 1972 has a pipe for a handle.
- This large mug of Catherine of Aragon, King Henry's first wife, has a castle tower for a handle.

Ann Bolyen — Mr.. Pickwick — Sir John Falstaff

49 SOME RECOGNIZABLE PERSONALITIES ARE IN THIS GROUP OF MUGS.

- King Henry's second wife was the unfortunate Anne Boleyn. As the song goes, "With her head tucked underneath her arm, she walked the bloody tower." An axe is the mug's handle.

- Mr. Samuel Pickwick was a fictional character created by Charles Dickens in his first book, *The Pickwick Papers*. He was the founder of the Pickwick Club.

- This small mug depicts the full body of Sir John Falstaff, but only the head. William Shakespeare eulogizes him in his fourth play.

Yachtsman — Night watchman — Porthos

50 THIS GROUPING HAS TWO NORMAL CHARACTERS AND ONE FICTIONAL.

- The Yachtsman, a large Royal Doulton mug, was created in 1970. Its Toby character has a sailboat for a handle.

- This Night Watchman vintage Royal Doulton character jug is extra-large with a street light for a handle.

- The Shakespearean character of Porthos is created in this Royal Dalton mug. It portrays one of the Three Musketeers, who enjoys wine, women, and song. This Toby character has a sword for a handle.

51 I CLOSE MY COLLECTION WITH A FEW WORDS ABOUT BEER CONTAINERS.

Growler – Neptune

- Beginning as early as the 1800s, people would bring their beer home in tin pails and glass jars or jugs from the local pubs. These jugs were called *growlers*. Supposedly the beer would slosh around, causing the carbon dioxide to escape and create a growling noise. This could be a myth or a true story, but the truth may never be known. I favor the noisy carbon dioxide story. A lot of brewers today still put their beer in growlers. This one I got from Marietta Brewing company in Marietta, Ohio.

- Lastly, I present Neptune, or as he was called in Roman religion 5,000 years ago, King Neptune. The counterpart in Greek tradition is Poseidon. King Neptune is the brother of Jupiter and Pluto and resides over the realms of heaven, the earthly world, and the underworld.

FINITE

I have learned a lot reviewing my collection, yet it's only a drop in the tin bucket. There are entire stores selling mugs, but to me having picked them up in my travels, looking back on those travels and remembering the stories is a true pleasure. The steins were not really a product of my travels. They mostly came out of receiving Avon or Budweiser steins. The Toby mugs started with a wedding gift from my wife's aunt in England.

As I said in the beginning, it is my *abridged* story.

I really took my collection for granted, but many friends said it was unique. Then my cousin suggested that I should make it my second book. I do not know if she was joking or not, but the more I thought about it, the more I liked the idea.

I have found the old adage, "You should never go back," has some truth. For example, it is sad to realize that some of these places to which I traveled are gone. For example, Treasure Island no longer puts on its pirate show in the lagoon out in front of its casino, The Mirage. The Blue Hole is closed to the public and just owned by a fishing club.

The Freedom Train toured all forty-eight contiguous United States and had more than seven million American visitors. The last visitor went through the train on December 31, 1977. The National Museums of Canada bought fifteen cars and from 1978 to 1980 toured across Canada as Discovery Trains, a mobile museum focusing on that country's history. The train now has a permanent home at the Baltimore and Ohio Railroad Museum in Baltimore, Maryland.

Route 66 is only a legend of being the *mother road*.

The windjammer, Polynesia, has been returned to Portugal as the Argus. The Sears Tower is now the Willis Tower and owned by Blackstone.

The five cent beer was a thing of the past even before I got this mug. Harvard Beer was gone before I even started working where it used to be.

The Prince of Fundy is running as the Fast Cat, but it might soon be gone because of COVID-19.

Most of the other mug locations are still there.

52 This last picture shows how I display my mugs and steins around the room. I still look at all of them as proof I was really there.

As Ernest Hemingway once said: "In order to write about life, you must first live it."

How I display the mugs
This is one of the four walls

The Mug

A cup with a handle throughout history
What it held never a mystery.

Mostly beer, sometimes ports.
In a hovel or the strongest forts.

At a soldier's side carried by his belt,
Always there, rarely felt.

Held by a handle,
By day or by candle.

To serve the beverage from a jug,
For a gentleman or a thug.

Whether he drank from a tap,
Listened to country or enjoyed rap.

In England drank with a toast,
To a companion or the host.

Lift the mug and call out cheers,
To relieve your worries or your fears.

Some are big; some are small,
Some are short; some are tall.

How different they can be,
Like a lake or a sea.

It could be glass,
Or earthenware from the past.

The Pilgrim's mug is made from leather,
What did the Indians use that sported a feather?

CPSIA information can be obtained
at www.ICGtesting.com
Printed in the USA
BVHW020515130721
611799BV00001B/5